FROM PAST TO PRESENT

How can our traditions and the traditions of others make our lives more interesting?

Literature

page 18

READING ACROSS TEXTS

Related Readings and Projects

page 4

So Will I

by Charlotte Zolotow

My grandfather remembers long ago
the white Queen Anne's lace that grew wild.
He remembers the buttercups and goldenrod
from when he was a child.

He remembers long ago
the white snow falling falling.
He remembers the bluebird and thrush
at twilight
calling, calling.

He remembers long ago
the new moon in the summer sky
He remembers the wind in the trees
and its long, rising sigh.
And so will I
        so will I.

Celebrate Traditions

In "So Will I" the author describes her grandfather's memories. Sharing memories is one part of having traditions. Traditions are beliefs, customs, and stories that have lasted over time. They may be family traditions, such as Sunday dinners at Grandma's house and stories about their growing-up years that parents tell children. Or they may be cultural traditions, such as holidays and special types of food and clothing.

Create a display to show the traditions that you celebrate. Follow these steps:

Gather Information

1. Think about traditions. Ask yourself: What special traditions does my family celebrate? What special traditions do my community, state, and nation celebrate? Make a list.

2. Find out about these traditions. Ask family members or use reference books and magazines. Make notes on your research.

Organize and Draw Conclusions

3. Put your notes on each tradition into its own group. For each tradition ask yourself: What objects or scenes could I gather or draw to help show this tradition?

4. Gather your objects and make your drawings.

Write and Present

5. For each tradition, write a short explanation of what it is and when and why people celebrate it. Put your objects, drawings, and explanations into a display. Share your display with the class.

Big Moon Tortilla

By Joy Cowley • Illustrated by Dyanne Strongbow

By the time Marta Enos had finished her homework, the sky was orange with sunset, and a fussing wind was blowing across the desert.

Marta Enos opened her window and looked outside.

In the cookhouse, Grandmother was making tortillas for the church supper. She slapped them into large circles and tossed them onto the iron plate over the mesquite fire. Grandmother's big moon tortillas were the best in the world!

The head of Marta Enos was filled with the knowing of fresh tortillas. Oh, that sweet, crisp, little-bit-burnt smell! It went to Marta's stomach, which rumbled and growled, and then on down to her feet, making her toes twitch towards the cookhouse.

The legs of Marta Enos would not wait another minute. They were in such a hurry to run to the cookhouse that they knocked over Marta's table, and that is when a disaster happened.

The homework papers with their neat writing and beautiful drawings went out the window and onto the breath of the fussing wind.

The wind huffed the papers high into the air. Then, with a little cough, it spread them over the village.

The legs of Marta Enos were sorry for their mistake, and they ran out to chase the homework papers, which slipped and slid like kites without string.

But the dogs, too, were chasing. Leaping into the air, they barked to each other, A game! A game!

In no time at all, the beautiful homework papers were torn and chewed into trash.

The second disaster happened when Marta tried to pull a page away from a puppy. Her glasses fell off, and she stepped on them. One arm of her glasses broke in half.

She did not smell tortillas anymore. Her head was filled up to her eyes with grief and tears as hot as chili peppers. Ruined homework! Broken glasses! Marta Enos ran to Grandmother.

Grandmother left her tortillas and sat down, as big as a bed and warm from the cooking. As she smoothed Marta's hair with her floured hands, she said, "Hush! Hush! If you cry so much you'll put out the fire."

"The dogs ate my homework, and I can't see to do any more!" Marta sobbed.

Grandmother rocked her. "Little problems," she said. "Too small for a big rainstorm. We'll repair your eyeglasses."

But the tears of Marta Enos still ran through her eyes and nose and made hiccups in her throat.

So Grandmother sang to her an old healing song, and with the healing song there was a story.

"When we have a problem we must choose what we will be. Sometimes it is good to be a tree, to stand up tall in the desert and look all ways at once."

"Sometimes it is best to be a rock, to sit very still, seeing nothing and saying nothing."

"Sometimes when you have a problem, you have to be a strong mountain lion, fierce and ready to fight for what is right."

"Sometimes the wisest thing is to be an eagle and fly. When the eagle is high up, it sees how small the earth is. It sees how small the problem is, and it laughs and laughs.

Grandmother wound some tape around the arm of the glasses. She put the glasses back on the nose and ears of Marta Enos. "That should be OK until we get them fixed," she said. "Now, one tortilla before supper?"

Grandmother pinched a ball of dough and slapped it between her hands, flip-flap, flip-flap, flip-flap. When it was as big and pale as a rising full moon, she dropped it onto the iron plate above the red-hot coals of the fire.

Ah, the smell as the tortilla bubbled and browned!

"I have decided," said Marta Enos, her legs doing a tortilla dance. "I am going to be the eagle."

Grandmother nodded. "That is very wise," she said, turning the tortilla over. "Fly high and laugh. Then come back and do your homework."

It's Only Human

In *Big Moon Tortilla,* Grandmother gives Marta advice about dealing with problems:

• Be a tree. Stand up tall in the desert and look all ways at once.

• Be an eagle and fly. See how small the problem is and laugh.

But trees can't really look around them, and eagles can't really laugh. Grandmother says these things to make a point. To make her point, she describes objects and animals as if they were human. This is called *personification.* Use personification to give some advice of your own.

What You Do

1. Think about how the second sentence might end: *When we have a problem, we must choose what to be. Sometimes it is good to be a . . .*

2. List at least three objects or animals to complete the sentence. For each object or animal, use personification to give your advice. Write at least two sentences for each piece of advice, like the examples at the top of the page.

3. Illustrate your personifications. Share your work with classmates.

Use What You Learn

4. Look over your results and the results of classmates. Work together to make a class book of advice. Share your book with other classes.

Holidays
Make Your Own!

Think about some of the holidays that you and your family celebrate. Then create an original idea for your own holiday. For example, how could you celebrate a half-birthday, or the middle of the school year? Make a poster to promote your new holiday.

What You Need
posterboard
(optional) construction paper
pencil, crayons, or markers
scissors
glue stick

What You Do
1. Brainstorm a few original holiday ideas and jot them down. Choose the idea you like best.
2. Think of ways that you could celebrate one of these holidays. Be sure to include any special costumes that you might wear, songs that you could sing, foods that you would prepare, and so on.
3. Make a poster about your original holiday. On the poster you could include words to a holiday song, a recipe for some special holiday food, a holiday poem, and so on. Share your poster with classmates.

Use What You Learn
4. Get together with classmates and discuss your posters. Which of these holidays would you like to celebrate and why?

Follow The Drinking Gourd

Story and Pictures by Jeanette Winter

Long ago,
before the Civil War,
there was an old sailor called Peg Leg Joe
who did what he could to help free the slaves.
Joe had a plan.
He'd use hammer and nail and saw
and work for the master, the man
who owned slaves
on the cotton plantation.
Joe had a plan.
At night when work was done,
he'd teach the slaves a song
that secretly told the way
to freedom.
Just follow the drinking gourd, it said.
When the song was learned
and sung all day,
Peg Leg Joe would slip away
to work for another master
and teach the song again.

One day
a slave called Molly saw her man James
sold to another master.
James would be taken away,
their family torn apart.
Just one more night together.
A quail called in the trees that night.
Molly and James remembered Joe's song.
They sang it low.

When the sun comes back, and the first quail calls,
Follow the drinking gourd.
For the old man is a-waiting for to carry you to freedom
If you follow the drinking gourd.

They looked to the sky and saw the stars.
Taking their little son Isaiah,
old Hattie, and her grandson George,
Molly and James set out for freedom
that very night,
following the stars of the drinking gourd.

They ran all night through the fields,
till they crossed the stream to the woods.
When daylight came, they hid in the trees,
watching,
listening
for the master's hounds
set loose to find them.
But the dogs lost the runaways' scent
at the stream,
and Molly and James and Isaiah,
old Hattie and young George,
were not found.
They hid all day in the woods.
At night they walked again, singing Joe's song
and looking for the signs
that marked the trail.

The riverbank makes a very good road,
The dead trees will show you the way.
Left foot, peg foot, traveling on,
Follow the drinking gourd.

Walking by night, sleeping by day,
for weeks they traveled on.
Sometimes berries to pick
and corn to snatch,
sometimes fish to catch,
sometimes empty bellies to sleep on.
Sometimes no stars to guide the way.
They never knew what lay ahead.
There was danger from men
who would send them back,
and danger from hungry beasts.
But sometimes a kind deed was done.
One day as they hid in a thicket
a boy from a farm found them.
In a bag of feed for the hogs in the wood
he brought bacon and corn bread to share.
Singing low, they traveled on.

The river ends between two hills,
Follow the drinking gourd.
There's another river on the other side,
Follow the drinking gourd.

On and on they followed the trail
to the river's end.
From the top of the hill they saw the new path,
another river beneath the stars
to lead them to freedom land.
The drinking gourd led them on.
The song was almost done.

When the great big river meets the little river,
Follow the drinking gourd.
For the old man is a-waiting for to carry you to freedom
If you follow the drinking gourd.

Then they climbed the last hill.
Down below was Peg Leg Joe
waiting at the wide Ohio River
to carry them across.

Their spirits rose when they saw the old man.
Molly and James and Isaiah, old Hattie and George,
ran to the shore.
Under a starry sky
Joe rowed them across the wide Ohio River.
He told them of hiding places
where they would be safe.
A path of houses stretched like a train
on a secret track leading north to Canada.
He called it the Underground Railroad.
It carried riders to freedom.
The first safe house stood on the hill.
The lamp was lit,
which meant it was safe to come.
Ragged and weary, they waited
while Joe signaled low, with a hoot like an owl.
Then the door opened wide
to welcome the freedom travelers.

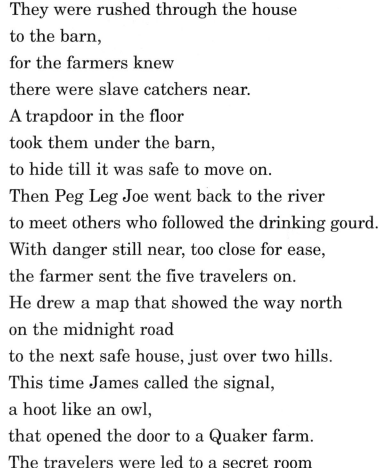

They were rushed through the house
to the barn,
for the farmers knew
there were slave catchers near.
A trapdoor in the floor
took them under the barn,
to hide till it was safe to move on.
Then Peg Leg Joe went back to the river
to meet others who followed the drinking gourd.
With danger still near, too close for ease,
the farmer sent the five travelers on.
He drew a map that showed the way north
on the midnight road
to the next safe house, just over two hills.
This time James called the signal,
a hoot like an owl,
that opened the door to a Quaker farm.
The travelers were led to a secret room
hidden behind shelves.
They rested here for many days
and healed their wounds.
Soft beds, full meals, new clothes, hot baths,
washed away some fear and pain.
Isaiah smiled.

When they were strong, they traveled again
from house to house on the underground trail,
still following the drinking gourd north.
Sometimes they traveled on foot,
sometimes by cart.
The wagon they rode near their journey's end
carried fruit to market
and the runaways to freedom.
At last they came to the shores of Lake Erie.
Molly and James and Isaiah,
old Hattie and young George,
climbed aboard the steamship
that would carry them across
to Canada, to freedom.
"Five more souls are safe!"
old Hattie cried.
The sun shone bright when they stepped on land.
They had followed the drinking gourd.

CHORUS

Fol-low ___ the drink-ing gourd! Fol-low ___ the

drink-ing gourd. ___ For the old man is a-wait-ing for to

car-ry you to free-dom If you fol-low the drink-ing gourd. *VERSE* When the

sun comes back, and the first quail calls, ___ Fol-low ___ the

drink-ing gourd. ___ For the old man is a-wait-ing for to

car-ry you to free-dom If you fol-low the drink-ing gourd.

(Repeat chorus)
The riverbank makes a very good road,
The dead trees will show you the way.
Left foot, peg foot, traveling on,
Follow the drinking gourd.

(Repeat chorus)
The river ends between two hills,
Follow the drinking gourd.
There's another river on the other side,
Follow the drinking gourd.

(Repeat chorus)
When the great big river meets the little river,
Follow the drinking gourd.
For the old man is a-waiting for to carry you to freedom
If you follow the drinking gourd.

THE UNDERGROUND RAILROAD

The slaves in *Follow the Drinking Gourd* make their way to freedom on the Underground Railroad—but no one ever gets on a train. The Underground Railroad was a group of people who helped slaves escape from the South to the North and to Canada.

Why was this system known as the Underground Railroad? It was called underground because people had to work in secret—it was against the law for slaves to run away from their masters. It was called a railroad because rescuers used railway terms as a kind of code to talk about their secret actions. The freed slaves were "freight," the routes were "lines," the stopping places for the slaves were "stations," and the people who helped the slaves along the lines were "conductors."

The Underground Railroad was a huge system that helped many slaves. Some believe that up to 100,000 slaves "traveled on the railroad" to freedom. But it was not easy. Slaves who left southern Alabama or Mississippi in the winter sometimes didn't arrive at the Ohio River until a year later—if they were not caught first.

The Underground Railroad followed many routes from the South to the North. Once in the North, the routes led to places where slaves could easily escape to Canada. Some of these ports were Detroit, Michigan; Sandusky, Ohio; Erie, Pennsylvania; and Buffalo, New York.

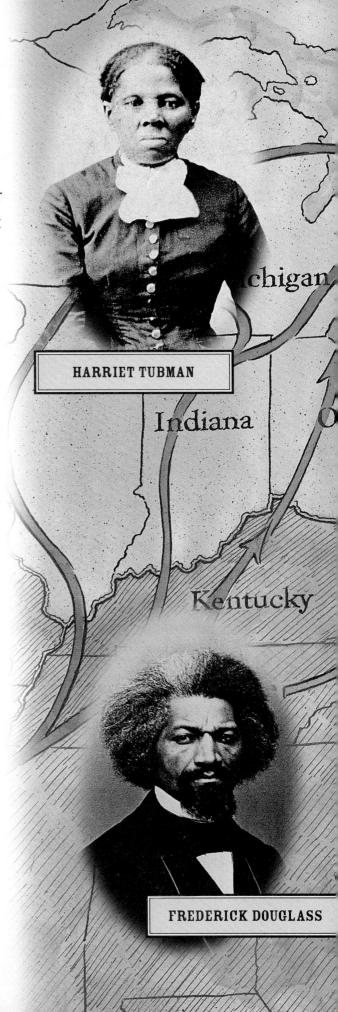

HARRIET TUBMAN

FREDERICK DOUGLASS

New York

ake Erie

Pennsylvania

Virginia

JOHN BROWN

North
Carolina

South
Carolina

Many people were involved in the Underground Railroad and fought against slavery. Two of the most famous rescuers were Harriet Tubman, who was known as the Moses of her people, and Levi Coffin. Frederick Douglass was an escaped slave who spoke out against slavery. John Brown also worked to free slaves. Lucretia Mott worked for both the rights of women and freedom for slaves. She and her husband made their home a "station" for the Underground Railroad.

TEACH ABOUT THE UNDERGROUND RAILROAD

Imagine that you are going to teach classmates about the Underground Railroad. What do you think they would need to know to understand it? You might try one of these ideas, or an idea of your own.

• Find out about one of the people who fought against slavery. Draw a picture of the person and write a paragraph or two that tells what that person did to help slaves.

• Pretend you are this person. Introduce yourself to classmates and explain your feelings about slavery and what you have done to help slaves.

• Use a reference source to find the routes. Trace the outline of a map and draw the routes on the map, marking major stopping points. Use a mileage scale to figure out the distances between major cities along one of the routes. Display your map and tell your classmates about one of the routes.

Crack the Code

The song "Follow the Drinking Gourd" is a secret code that helped slaves escape without their owners knowing when and where they were going. The song would help the slaves remember what path to take to freedom. Here is the code and what it means.

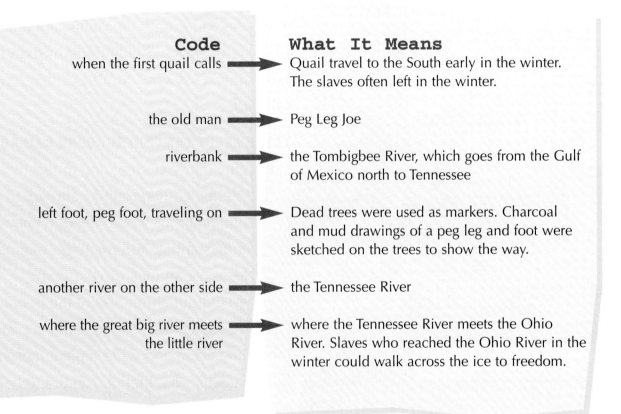

Code	What It Means
when the first quail calls ➜	Quail travel to the South early in the winter. The slaves often left in the winter.
the old man ➜	Peg Leg Joe
riverbank ➜	the Tombigbee River, which goes from the Gulf of Mexico north to Tennessee
left foot, peg foot, traveling on ➜	Dead trees were used as markers. Charcoal and mud drawings of a peg leg and foot were sketched on the trees to show the way.
another river on the other side ➜	the Tennessee River
where the great big river meets the little river ➜	where the Tennessee River meets the Ohio River. Slaves who reached the Ohio River in the winter could walk across the ice to freedom.

Make Your Own Code

Notice that in a code, the two sides are equivalent. One thing equals another. Make up a code of your own. In your code, you could have numbers or pictures equal letters or words.

After you make your code, use it to write a message. Imagine that a friend asks you how to get from one place to another. Write your answer in code. Share your code with relatives and friends. See whether they can figure it out.

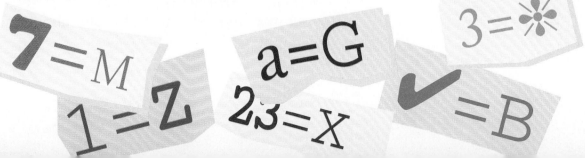

It's Written in the STARS

The drinking gourd mentioned in the song is the Big Dipper, a pattern of stars called a constellation. The Big Dipper is always above the horizon, so people who live in the northern half of the world can see it all year. What constellations can you see from where you live? Make a poster about a constellation you would be able to see from your town.

What You Need

• a book about constellations   • posterboard   • crayons or markers

What You Do

1. Find a constellation and draw it. Connect the stars with lines to show the shape they make.

2. Attach cards with the name of your constellation and other information. You might write the story or legend about the group of stars, tell how ancient sailors or farmers used the constellation, and so on.

Use What You Know

3. On a smaller piece of paper, draw your constellation and the ones your classmates drew. Go outside on a clear night and look for the constellations. Which ones can you find? Are they in the middle of the sky? Are they near the horizon? Do they change location from one night to the next?

Reader Response

1. Think About the Theme

How can our traditions and the traditions of others make our lives more interesting? As you write the answer to this question, think about the selections you've read and about your own family or community.

2. Ask a Question

What questions do you have about the Underground Railroad? If you could talk to Peg Leg Joe, what would you ask him? List at least five questions. Where could you find the answers to your questions?

3. Use New Vocabulary

Make a list of new words you learned from these selections. Write definitions or draw pictures that illustrate each word. See if classmates can figure out which words you are describing.

4. Make Connections

Compare and contrast the ways the authors presented traditions in *Big Moon Tortilla* and "So Will I."

5. Analyze

What do you admire most about Peg Leg Joe? What would you have done if you were in his position? What other characters like him have you read or heard about? Write about these characters.